# CLEAN WATER ACT
# WATER QUALITY DESIGNATED USES AND IMPAIRMENTS

## Dinosaur National Monument

Technical Report NPS/NRWRD/NRTR-2003/306

March 2003

National Park Service
Water Resources Division
Fort Collins, Colorado

The National Park Service Water Resources Division is responsible for providing water resources management policy and guidelines, planning, technical assistance, training, and operational support to units of the National Park System. Program areas include water rights, water resources planning, regulatory guidance and review, hydrology, water quality, watershed management, watershed studies, and aquatic ecology.

**Technical Reports**

The National Park Service disseminates the results of biological, physical, and social research through the Natural Resources Technical Series. Natural resources inventories and monitoring activities, scientific literature reviews, bibliographies, and proceedings of technical workshops and conferences are also disseminated through this series.

Mention of trade names or commercial products does not constitute endorsement or recommendation for use by the National Park Service.

Digital copies of this and other completed park reports are available at http://www.nature.nps.gov/wrd. Clean Water Act designated use and impairment GIS shapefiles generated during the preparation of this and other park reports may also be found at this website along with a searchable database of park hydrographic statistics.

Analog copies of this report are available from the following:

Technical Information Center            (303) 969-2130
Denver Services Center
P.O. Box 25287
Denver, CO  80225-0287

U.S. Department of Commerce             (703) 487-4650
National Technical Information Center
5285 Port Royal Road
Springfield, VA  22161

# CLEAN WATER ACT
# WATER QUALITY DESIGNATED USES AND IMPAIRMENTS

## for

## DINOSAUR NATIONAL MONUMENT

Technical Report NPS/NRWRD/NRTR-2003/306

March 2003

National Park Service
Water Resources Division
Fort Collins, Colorado

# EXECUTIVE SUMMARY

Director's Order NPS-75 requires the National Park Service (NPS) Natural Resource Inventory and Monitoring Program to establish a Servicewide inventory of waterbodies and water quality use classifications. The Government Performance and Results Act of 1993 (GPRA) directs Federal agencies to articulate program goals in a quantifiable and measurable manner. These mandates are reflected in the mission goals of the 2000 NPS Strategic Plan. Included among these mission goals are the creation of a water resources inventory and achieving a target of 85% of 265 park units with unimpaired waterbodies. To help achieve the goals of NPS-75, GPRA, and the NPS Strategic Plan, this report summarizes for Dinosaur National Monument (DINO): (1) Clean Water Act (CWA) State-designated uses; (2) CWA 303(d) quality impaired waters and causes; (3) special designations recognizing waters of exceptional quality as defined in State water quality standards; and (4) hydrographic statistics based on the United States Geological Survey (USGS) 1:100,000 scale National Hydrography Dataset (NHD). Data sources used to compile this report include: Environmental Protection Agency (EPA) Total Maximum Daily Load Tracking System, EPA Water Quality Standards Database, EPA National Assessment Database, EPA EnviroMapper for Water, USGS NHD, the Colorado Department of Public Health and Environment – Water Quality Control Division, and the Utah Department of Environmental Quality – Division of Water Quality.

Based on the NHD, a total of 540.27 miles of perennial and intermittent streams, 4.68 acres of lakes and ponds, and 34 springs/seeps are within or adjacent to the DINO park boundary. Colorado State-designated uses for classified waterbodies within or adjacent to the DINO park boundary include: (1) agriculture; (2) aquatic life cold water – class 1; (3) aquatic life warm water - class 2; (4) domestic water source; (5) recreation primary contact; and (6) recreation secondary contact. Utah State-designated uses for classified waterbodies within or adjacent to the DINO park boundary include: (1) agriculture; (2) cold water game fish; (3) drinking water supply; (4) secondary contact (recreation); and (5) warm water game fish. No waterbodies within or adjacent to the DINO park boundary are impaired based on the 2002 Colorado and 2002 Utah 303(d) list. No Outstanding National Resource Waters or Outstanding State Resource Water designations have been applied to waters within or adjacent to the DINO park boundary in Colorado. The Green River and Jones Hole Creek with tributaries have been designated by the State of Utah as Outstanding National Resource Waters.

# TABLE OF CONTENTS

# LIST OF TABLES

# LIST OF FIGURES

# INTRODUCTION

The National Park Service's (NPS) Organic Act of 1916 and the Clean Water Act (CWA) are two important pieces of federal legislation that provide for the preservation, conservation, and protection of water resources within units of the National Park System. The mission of the Organic Act states that "the Service thus established shall promote and regulate the use of Federal areas known as national parks, monuments and reservations . . . by such means and measures as conform to the fundamental purpose of the said parks, monuments and reservations, which purpose is to conserve the scenery and the natural and historic objects and the wild life therein and to provide for the enjoyment of the same in such manner and by such means as will leave them unimpaired for the enjoyment of future generations" (16 U.S.C. Section 1). The stated objective of the CWA is to "restore and maintain the chemical, physical and biological integrity of the nation's waters" (33 U.S.C. Section 1251(a)).

To help meet its resource stewardship responsibilities the NPS established the Natural Resource Inventory and Monitoring (I&M) Program. The goal of the I&M Program is to acquire the information and expertise needed by park managers to maintain ecosystem integrity in the approximately 270 National Park System units that contain significant natural resources (National Park Service 2000a). The establishment of a Servicewide natural resource inventory, which is to include a water resources inventory, is an important objective of the I&M Program. The 1992 Director's Order NPS-75, *Natural Resources and Inventory Monitoring Guideline*, recommends the water resources inventory include: (1) location (with additional classification from that included in digital cartographic information) of streams, lakes, wetlands, and groundwater (hot springs, cold springs); and (2) water quality use classifications (Ibid, 26).

The Government Performance and Results Act of 1993 (GPRA) directs Federal agencies to articulate program goals in a quantifiable and measurable manner. GPRA requires the use of strategic plans, annual performance plans, and annual performance reports for Federal programs (Galvin 1999). The 2000 NPS Strategic Plan reflects the mandates of NPS-75 and GPRA in its mission goals. Included in these goals are the creation of a water resources inventory (mission goal Ib1) and achieving a target of 85% of 265 park units with unimpaired waters (mission goal Ia4) (National Park Service 2000b, 17, 20).

## Purposes

The purposes of this report are to compile and summarize the following for Dinosaur National Monument (DINO): (1) CWA State-designated use classifications; (2) CWA 303(d) quality impaired waters and causes; (3) special designations recognizing waters of exceptional quality as defined in State water quality standards; and (4) hydrographic statistics based on the United States Geological Survey (USGS) 1:100,000 scale National Hydrography Dataset (NHD). This report provides the water quality use classifications for park waterbodies as directed by NPS-75 and the I&M Strategic Plan (National Park Service 1993). Although hydrographic statistics are presented in the report, it is important to note that these were generated from the 1:100,000-scale (medium resolution) NHD, which is complete for the entire country. It is anticipated that the I&M Program will acquire 1:24,000-scale (high resolution) NHD for parks to provide the definitive locations and inventory of streams, lakes, rivers, and other hydrographic features. This effort, however, will likely take several years.

## Dinosaur National Monument Environs and Overview

DINO is located along the northern Colorado/Utah State border in the Upper Green – Flaming Gorge Reservoir, Lower Yampa, Lower White, Lower Green – Diamond, and Ashley - Brush subbasins[1] (Figure 1). Based on the NHD, a total of 540.27 miles of perennial and intermittent streams, 4.68 acres of lakes and ponds, and 34 springs/seeps are within or adjacent to the DINO park boundary (Table I). Colorado State-designated uses for classified waterbodies within or adjacent to the DINO park boundary include: (1) agriculture; (2) aquatic life cold water – class 1; (3) aquatic life warm water - class 2; (4) domestic water source; (5) recreation primary contact; and (6) recreation secondary contact (Table II and Figures 3-4). Utah State-designated uses for classified waterbodies within or adjacent to the DINO park boundary include: (1) agriculture; (2) cold water game fish; (3) drinking water supply; (4) secondary contact (recreation); and (5) warm water game fish (Table III and Figure 2). No waterbodies within or adjacent to the DINO park boundary are impaired based on the 2002 Colorado and 2000 Utah 303(d) list

---

[1] A subbasin is equivalent to the USGS cataloging unit identified by an 8-digit hydrologic unit code.

(Table IV). No Outstanding National Resource Waters (ONRWs) or Outstanding State Resource Water designations have been applied to waters within or adjacent to the DINO park boundary in Colorado. The Green River and Jones Hole Creek with tributaries have been designated by the State of Utah as Outstanding National Resource Waters.

# BACKGROUND

**Water Quality Standards**

An important component of the CWA is the requirement of water quality standards. Water quality standards are established by the States and consist of three elements: (1) designated use classifications; (2) numerical and/or narrative water quality criteria; and (3) an antidegradation policy (Environmental Protection Agency 1998, 5). The CWA requires all States to establish use classifications for all waterbodies within the State, *e.g.*, public drinking water supplies, propagation of fish and wildlife, recreational purposes, industrial, and other uses. Water quality criteria are numerical descriptions of the physical, chemical, and biological characteristics of waters necessary to support the designated uses (Gallagher and Miller 1996, 58).

**Federal Antidegradation Policies and Regulations**

The antidegradation policy as promulgated by the Environmental Protection Agency (EPA) in the Code of Federal Regulations at 40 C.F.R. Part 131.12 acts as a key portion of States' water quality standards by requiring, at a minimum, States to include provisions for the management of water quality in accordance with the following 'Tiers':

Tier 1: Includes the provisions to protect existing uses of water in the State, which constitute the absolute floor or minimum level of protection that must be provided all waters (Environmental Protection Agency 1993, 4-1).

Tier 2: Applies to waters whose quality exceeds that necessary to protect "fishable/swimmable" goals of the CWA. Management of these waters must attempt to keep them at existing quality. Degradation may be allowed if it cannot be avoided for social or economic development reasons, but only after public review has occurred (Ibid).

Tier 3: Applies to ONRWs where ordinary use classifications and supporting criteria may not be sufficient or appropriate. ONRWs are frequently considered the highest quality waters of the United States, but may also include waterbodies that are of "exceptional recreational or ecological significance," as stated under 40 C.F.R. Section 131.12(a)(3) of the antidegradation policy. ONRWs are afforded the highest level of protection under the antidegradation policy. Existing water quality is to be maintained and protected, and only activities that cause short-term and temporary degradation may be allowed (Environmental Protection Agency 1993, 4-10).

An additional concept of a Tier 2 ½ waterbody was developed by States out of a concern that the Tier 3 provision was too restrictive of social and economic development. A Tier 2 ½ waterbody, which the EPA does accept, offers more protection than a Tier 2 waterbody without the strict prohibition against the lowering of water quality found in the Tier 3 provision (Ibid, 4-2).

The National Park System encompasses some of the most sensitive, pristine, and significant aquatic resources in the United States. Many of these aquatic resources have been afforded the protection of Tier 2 ½ or Tier 3 ONRW status. Such exceptional waterbodies located within or adjacent to park boundaries shall be identified in this report.

**Colorado State Antidegradation Regulations**

Colorado's water quality standards and regulations are codified in Regulation No. 31 of the Colorado Code of Regulations (C.C.R.) at Title 5 C.C.R. 1002-31 (Basic Standards and Methodologies for Surface Water). The antidegradation provisions of Regulation No. 31 are summarized below as quoted from the 1998 Colorado Water Quality Management and Drinking Water Protection Handbook:

> The antidegradation provisions of the Basic Standards and Methodologies for Surface Water: (1)
> set forth provisions regarding the adoption of water quality-based designations for certain surface

waters; and (2) establish an antidegradation review process applicable to certain activities impacting the quality of surface waters. See generally, section 31.8.

Either of two water quality-based designations may be adopted in appropriate circumstances. Section 31.8(2). An "outstanding waters" designation may be applied to certain high quality waters that constitute an outstanding natural resource. No degradation of outstanding waters by regulated activities is allowed. A "use-protected waters" designation may be applied to waters with existing quality that is not better than necessary to support propagation of fish, shellfish, and wildlife and recreation in and on the water. The quality of these waters may be altered so long as applicable use-based water quality classifications and standards are met.

Waters that are not given one of these designations are subject to antidegradation review requirements before any new or increased water quality impacts are allowed. Section 31.8(3). The activities that are subject to these requirements are those that: (1) require a discharge permit; (2) require water quality certification under section 401 of the federal Act; or (3) are subject to control regulations. The first step in the antidegradation review process is a determination, in accordance with criteria specified in the regulation, whether "significant degradation" would result from the activity. If not, the review ceases. If significant degradation would result, a determination is made whether the degradation is necessary to accommodate important economic or social development in the area in which the waters are located. This determination is based on an assessment of whether there are quality control alternatives available that would result in less degradation of state waters and which are economically, environmentally, and technologically reasonable. The proposed degradation is allowed only if no such alternatives are available (Ibid, 34).

**Utah State Antidegradation Regulations**

Utah's water quality standards are codified at Rule R317-2 of the Utah Administrative Code (U.A.C.). The antidegradation provision of Utah's water quality standards provide for the maintenance of water quality and the establishment of three categories of high quality waters. The following quote from R317-2-3 establishes the maintenance of water quality:

> Waters whose existing quality is better than the established standards for the designated uses will be maintained at high quality unless it is determined by the Board, after appropriate intergovernmental coordination and public participation in concert with the Utah continuing planning process, allowing lower water quality is necessary to accommodate important economic or social development in the area in which the waters are located. However, existing instream water uses shall be maintained and protected. No water quality degradation is allowable which would interfere with or become injurious to existing instream water uses (R317-2-3, U.A.C.).

Utah has three categories of high quality waters for which special protection is provided. Category 1 waters are analogous to the Tier 3 designation and are defined in R317-2-3 as "waters of high quality which have been determined by the Board to be of exceptional recreational or ecological significance or have been determined to be a State or National resource requiring protection...." Category 2 waters are analogous to the Tier 2 ½ designation and are essentially Category 1 waters with the caveat that point source discharges may be permitted provided that the discharge does not degrade existing water quality. Category 3 waters relates primarily to drinking water sources and provides for extra evaluation of new point source discharges relative to Category 2. Utah does not have any formal list for Tier 1 and Tier 2 waterbodies (River Network 2002).

**303(d) Waterbodies and Total Maximum Daily Loads**

Waterbodies that fail to comply with standards are compiled by States into a list, commonly referred to as "303(d) lists" after the section of the CWA which contains the requirement, for submittal to the EPA. The EPA approves the list only if it meets applicable requirements. Waterbodies on an approved 303(d) list require the establishment of a total maximum daily load (TMDL) (Environmental Protection Agency 2002a). A TMDL specifies the amount of a particular pollutant that may be present in a waterbody, allocates allowable pollutant loads among sources, and provides the basis for attaining or maintaining water quality standards (65 Fed. Reg. 43588 (July 13, 2000)). For the purposes of this report, a 303(d) listed waterbody is considered impaired.

**Waterbodies (Waters of the United States)**

The term "waterbodies" is used in this report with the same meaning the EPA applies to the term "navigable waters." "Navigable waters" are defined in the CWA to include all "waters of the United States." The term "waters of the United States" is defined in Title 40 C.F.R. Part 122.2 as:

> (a) All waters which are currently used, were used in the past, or may be susceptible to use in interstate or foreign commerce, including all waters which are subject to the ebb and flow of the tide; (b) All interstate waters, including interstate "wetlands;" (c) All other waters such as intrastate lakes, rivers, streams (including intermittent streams), mudflats, sandflats, "wetlands," sloughs, prairie potholes, wet meadows, playa lakes, or natural ponds the use, degradation, or destruction of which would affect or could affect interstate or foreign commerce including any such waters: (1) Which are or could be used by interstate or foreign travelers for recreational or other purposes; (2) From which fish or shellfish are or could be taken and sold in interstate or foreign commerce; or (3) Which are used or could be used for industrial purposes by industries in interstate commerce; (d) All impoundments of waters otherwise defined as waters of the United States under this definition; (e) Tributaries of waters identified in paragraphs (a) through (d) of this definition; (f) The territorial sea; and (g) "Wetlands" adjacent to waters (other than waters that are themselves wetlands) identified in paragraphs (a) through (f) of this definition.

Although not included in the above referenced definition, the EPA has also ruled that springs and seeps that support unusual flora or fauna which attract large numbers of out-of-state scientists are considered "waters of the United States" (Sullivan 1995, 139). Anthropogenic waste treatment systems, such as treatment ponds or lagoons, are not included as "waters of the United States."

**Waterbody Identifications and Reaches**

Water quality standard information in this report is linked to State-defined waterbody identification (WBID) codes. A WBID is a unique code, which represents the basic unit for reporting water quality standards to the EPA. States currently use a variety of methods for defining WBIDs, such as the use of individual monitoring stations and Natural Resource Conservation Service watersheds. The geographic extents for these WBIDs are occasionally defined by States using geographic information systems (GIS) but more often are only described textually (Environmental Protection Agency 2001, Appendix B).

A reach is a continuous, unbroken stretch or expanse of surface water. In the NHD, this idea has been expanded to define a reach as a significant segment of surface water that has similar hydrologic characteristics, such as a stretch of stream/river between two confluences, or a lake/pond (U.S. Geological Survey 2000a, 9). The EPA has strongly encouraged States to uniformly adopt the NHD reach addressing protocol for assigning WBIDs (Environmental Protection Agency 2001, Appendix B).

The geographic representation of water features in the NHD serves as a framework for organizing and integrating water quality attribute information under the EPA WATERS[2] system. Since relatively few States have adopted the NHD reach addressing protocol, the EPA is currently undergoing the process of georeferencing State WBIDs and other water quality program information to reaches in the NHD (Environmental Protection Agency 2002b). In other words, the EPA is assigning reach codes to State WBIDs so that they may be analyzed and displayed by computer-based tools, such as a GIS.

---

[2] WATERS (Watershed Assessment, Tracking & Environmental Results) unites water quality information that was previously available only from several independent and unconnected databases (*e.g.*, TMDL Tracking System and the Water Quality Standards Database). WATERS is located on the Internet at http://www.epa.gov/waters/.

A recent study prepared by the General Accounting Office (GAO) noted the difficulties the EPA faces when transferring State water quality data to the NHD in the WATERS system due to the number of different ways States define their waters. According to the GAO study, less than one-third of State water quality officials who were interviewed indicated that their States' water quality is reflected "somewhat" or "very" accurately in the WATERS system (General Accounting Office 2002, 28). Errors noted by the NPS during the preparation of this and similar reports included incomplete georeferencing and misidentifications of WBIDs. Although reasonable efforts were made to find and correct any errors originating from EPA georeferencing efforts, the NPS makes no expressed or implied guarantees regarding the depiction of WBIDs in this report.

# DATA SOURCES

Information used to compile this report was derived primarily from the following sources:

- **Water Quality Standards Database (WQSDB)** – The WQSDB is being developed by the EPA for the purpose of tracking water quality standards, including designated uses and numeric criteria, for the Nation's surface waters. The source information for the WQSDB is obtained from each State's water quality standards (WQS) regulations. For those States not currently included in the WQSDB, the full text of the WQS is made available on EPA's WQSDB website. The WQSDB can be visited at: http://www.epa.gov/wqsdatabase. For more information on the WQSDB, contact Bill Kramer at kramer.bill@epa.gov, (202) 260-5824, or at the following mailing address: 1200 Pennsylvania Avenue NW, Mailcode 4305T, Washington, DC 20460.

- **National Assessment Database (NAD)** - NAD contains information on the attainment of water quality standards. Assessed waters are classified as either Fully Supporting, Threatened, or Not Supporting their designated uses. This information is reported in the National Water Quality Inventory Report to Congress under Section 305(b) of the Clean Water Act. NAD can be visited at: http://www.epa.gov/waters/305b. For more information on NAD, contact Cary McElhinney at mcelhinney.cary@epa.gov, (202) 566-1188, or at the following mailing address: 1200 Pennsylvania Avenue NW, Mailcode 4503T, Washington, DC 20460.

- **TMDL Tracking System** – The EPA TMDL Tracking System contains information on all impaired waters under section 303(d) of the CWA. The database also has information on EPA approved TMDLs. The TMDL Tracking System can be visited at: http://www.epa.gov/waters/tmdl/trcksys.html. For more information on the TMDL Tracking System, contact Chris Laabs at laabs.chris@epa.gov, (202) 260-7030, or at the following mailing address: 1200 Pennsylvania Avenue NW, Mailcode 4503T, Washington, DC 20460.

- **EnviroMapper for Water** – EnviroMapper for Water is a web-based Geographic Information System application that dynamically displays information about bodies of water in the U.S. This interactive tool allows the creation of customized maps portraying the nation's surface waters along with a collection of environmental data. EnviroMapper can be visited at: http://www.epa.gov/waters/enviromapper. For more information on EnviroMapper, contact Cary McElhinney at mcelhinney.cary@epa.gov, (202) 566-1188, or at the following mailing address: 1200 Pennsylvania Avenue NW, Mailcode 4503T, Washington, DC 20460.

- **National Hydrography Dataset (NHD)** – The USGS NHD is a nationally consistent hydrography database for the United States. It combines elements of the USGS digital line graph (DLG) hydrography files and the EPA Reach File (RF3). The NHD contains unique reach identifiers, called reach codes, for each reach in the coverage. In addition to linear hydrography, the NHD contains points and areal (or polygonal) entities to represent features such as wells, springs, lakes, and reservoirs. The NHD with a 1:100,000 scale (medium resolution data) was used for this report. High resolution data (typically developed from 1:24,000 scale USGS topographic maps) are currently under development and are not available on a wide enough basis to be utilized for this project. The NHD can be visited at: http://nhd.usgs.gov. The NHD can be visited at: http://nhd.usgs.gov. For more information on the NHD, contact Paul Wiese at pmwiese@usgs.gov, (303) 202-4298, or at the following mailing address: P.O. Box 25046, MS 516, Denver, CO 80225-0046.

- **Colorado Department of Public Health and Environment – Water Quality Control Division (Colorado WQCD)** – The Colorado WQCD was contacted for further information on waterbody designated uses and impairments, as well as information on Outstanding National and State Resource Waters. The WQCD website can be accessed at: http://www.cpdhe.state.co.us/wq/wqhom.asp. For further information, contact Sarah Johnson at sarah.johnson@state.co.us, (303) 692-3500, or at the following mailing address: 4300 Cherry Creek Drive South, Denver, CO 80246-1530.

- **Utah Department of Environmental Quality – Division of Water Quality (Utah DEQ-DWQ)** – The Utah DWQ was contacted for further information on waterbody designated uses and impairments, as well as information on Outstanding National and State Resource Waters. The DWQ website can be accessed at: waterquality.utah.gov/. For further information, contact Tom Toole at ttoole@deq.state.ut.us, (801) 538-6859, or at the following mailing address: P.O. Box 144870, Salt Lake City, UT 84114-4870.

**Figure 1. Regional Location Map**

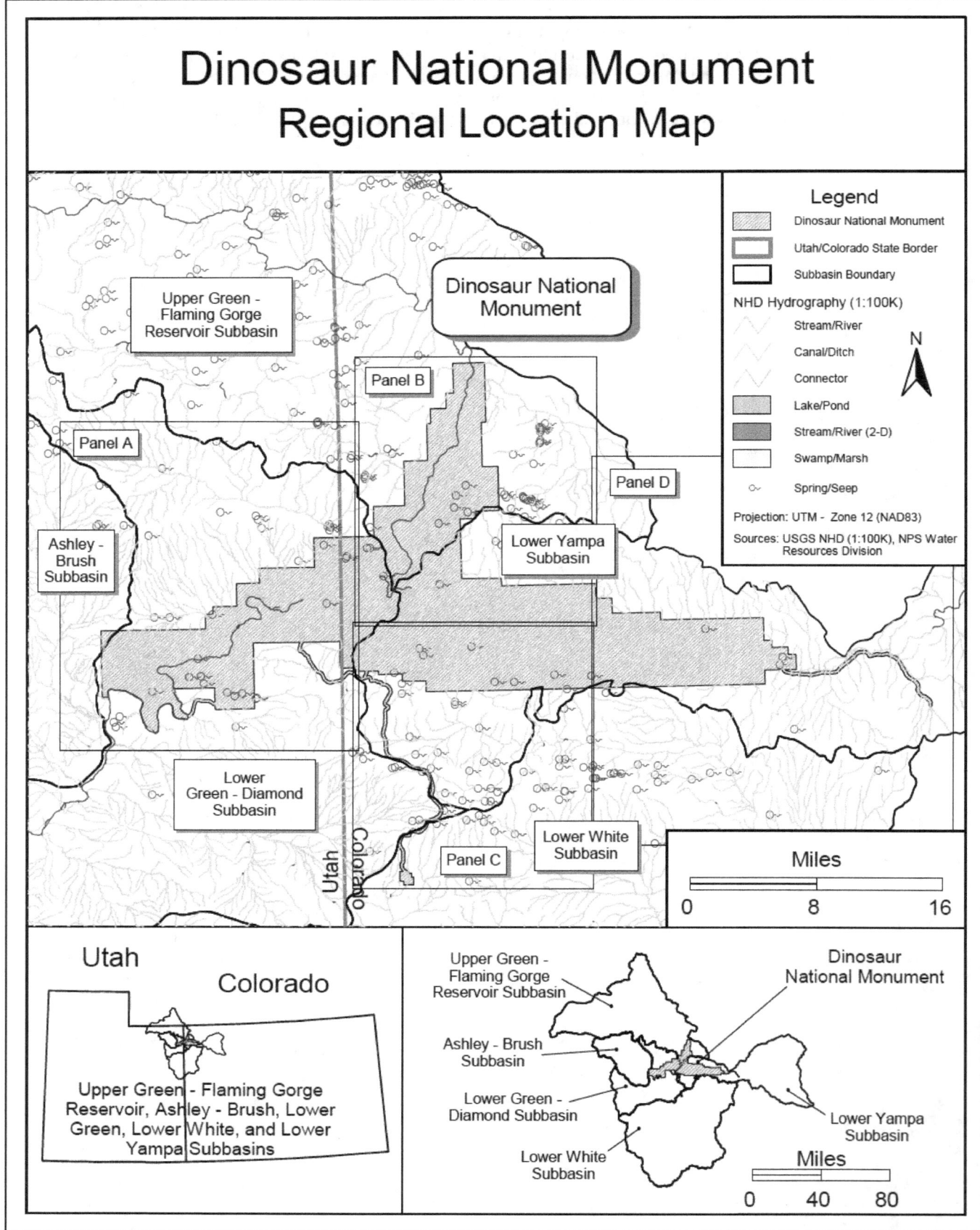

# PARK HYDROGRAPHIC STATISTICS

Table I summarizes statistics for areal, linear, and point hydrographic features within and adjacent to the DINO park boundary based on the USGS 1:100,000 scale NHD. Prior to running any statistical analyses on the DINO hydrography, the NHD and DINO park boundary shapefile were projected into the Universal Transverse Mercator (UTM) zone 15, North American Datum (NAD) 83 coordinate system. A subset of the NHD, consisting only of waterbodies found within or adjacent to the DINO park boundary, was generated using the ArcView Geoprocessing Wizard. The lengths and areas of the "clipped" dataset were finally calculated using the "Add Acres/Miles" option of the AlaskaPak ArcView extension.

The determination of what constituted an adjacent waterbody was a judgment call based on a review of the NHD, the park boundary shapefile, and 1:24,000 scale USGS topographical maps. In general, any waterbody that appeared to be contiguous with the park boundary was considered to be adjacent.

## Table I. Park Hydrographic Statistics

| AREAL HYDROGRAPHIC FEATURES (Based on the NHD Waterbody Theme) | | | | | |
|---|---|---|---|---|---|
| Feature Description | Hydrographic Category | Acres | % of Total | Shoreline Miles | % of Total |
| Stream/River (2-dimensional)[1] | Perennial | 1528.14 | 73.9 | -- | -- |
| Stream/River – Adjacent (2-dimensional)[1] | Perennial | 535.61 | 25.9 | -- | -- |
| Lake/Pond | Perennial | 4.68 | 0.2 | 0.5 | 100 |
| | Total | 2068.43 | | 0.5 | |

| LINEAR HYDROGRAPHIC FEATURES By Feature Description (Based on the NHD Network Element Theme) | | |
|---|---|---|
| Feature Description/Hydrographic Category | Miles | % of Total |
| Stream/River – Perennial[2] | 113.81 | 21.0 |
| Stream/River – Perennial[2] (Adjacent) | 13.40 | 2.5 |
| Stream/River – Intermittent | 413.06 | 76.0 |
| Canal/Ditch | 0.23 | 0.0 |
| Connector[3] | 0.81 | 0.1 |
| Artificial Path[4] | 1.73 | 0.3 |
| Artificial Path[4] (Adjacent) | 0.16 | 0.0 |
| Total[5] | 543.20 | |

| By Level (Based on the NHD Transport and Coastline Reach Theme) | | |
|---|---|---|
| Level[6] | Miles | % of Total |
| 4 | 45.81 | 8.4 |
| 4 (Adjacent) | 12.17 | 2.2 |
| 5 | 145.48 | 26.8 |
| 5 (Adjacent) | 0.15 | 0.0 |
| 6 | 199.98 | 36.8 |
| 7 | 112.66 | 20.7 |
| 8 | 14.83 | 2.7 |
| 9 | 0.41 | 0.1 |
| 10 | 0.84 | 0.2 |
| 11 | 0.10 | 0.1 |
| -9998 | 9.06 | 1.7 |
| -9998 (Adjacent) | 1.63 | 0.3 |
| Total[5] | 543.12 | |

| POINT HYDROGRAPHIC FEATURES (Based on the NHD Point Landmark Theme) | | |
|---|---|---|
| Feature Description | Count | % of Total |
| Spring/Seep | 34 | 100 |
| Total | 34 | |

*Notes*

[1] In the NHD stream/rivers are depicted as 1-dimensional lines or 2-dimensional waterbodies. A 2-dimensional waterbody in the NHD is a hydrographic feature that is delineated using areas (U.S. Geological Survey 2000a, 39).

[2] For the purpose of generating linear hydrographic statistics, the "Stream/River – Perennial" category incorporates the NHD feature type "artificial path" for those artificial paths located within a perennial 2-dimensional stream/river. An artificial path represents the flow of water into, through, and out of features delineated using areas (that is, it serves as a centerline) and also delineates the coastline (U.S. Geological Survey 2000a, 8).

[3] The connector serves the special function in NHD of helping to ensure that the hydrographic network is complete by filling the gaps in the delineation of other features (U.S. Geological Survey 2000a, 8).

[4] Artificial paths not representing centerlines or not located within 2-dimensional stream/rivers are accounted for here.

[5] Totals for linear hydrographic features may differ slightly due to rounding errors.

[6] Level – Stream level. Has a value range of 1 to 99 and the value –9998 for "unspecified" (U.S. Geological Survey 2000b, 9). Stream level is assigned by identifying the terminus of the drainage network. The lowest value for stream level is assigned to a transport reach at the end of a flow and to upstream transport reaches that trace the main path of flow back to the head. The stream level is incremented by one and is assigned to all transport reaches that terminate at this path (that is, all tributaries to the path) and to all transport reaches that trace the main path of the flow along each tributary back to its head. The stream level value is incremented again and is assigned to transport reaches that trace the main path of the tributaries to their heads. This process is continued until all transport reaches for which flow is encoded are assigned a stream level (U.S. Geological Survey 2000a, 18).

# DESIGNATED USES

Colorado waterbodies are classified according to the uses for which they are presently suitable or intended to become suitable. Classifications may be established for any of Colorado's waterbodies, except that water in ditches and other manmade conveyance structures shall not be classified (5 C.C.R 1002-31, 39). Colorado-designated beneficial use definitions for the waterbodies within or adjacent to the DINO park boundary are provided in Table II.

Utah waterbodies are grouped into classes as to protect against controllable pollution. Beneficial uses are designated within each waterbody class. Waterbodies not specifically classified are presumptively classified as 2B (secondary contact recreation) and 3D (warm water game fish) (R317-2, U.A.C.). Utah-designated beneficial use definitions for the waterbodies within or adjacent to the DINO park boundary are provided in Table III.

State-designated beneficial uses and use support information for waterbodies within or adjacent to the DINO park boundary are listed in Table IV[3]. Waterbody designated uses and impairment status are shown in Figure 2.

The State-designated uses and hydrographic statistics located in Table III are based on GIS WBID shapefiles provided for the NPS Water Resources Division by the EPA. State-designated use data provided by the State was used in lieu of the EPA data if the State data was more up-to-date or there was a discrepancy between the EPA and State data. Best professional judgment was used to edit the EPA provided WBID shapefiles if the shapefiles did not appear to correspond with the State's description of the WBID.

## Table II. Colorado-Designated Beneficial Use Definitions

| State - Designated Use Code | State-Designated Use | State-Designated Use Definition |
|---|---|---|
| AG | Agriculture | These surface waters are suitable or intended to become suitable for irrigation of crops usually grown in Colorado and which are not hazardous as drinking water for livestock. |
| ALCW1 | Aquatic Life Cold Water-Class 1 | These are waters that (1) currently are capable of sustaining a wide variety of cold water biota, including sensitive species, or (2) could sustain such biota but for correctable water quality conditions. Waters shall be considered capable of sustaining such biota where physical habitat, water flows or levels, and water quality conditions result in no substantial impairment of the abundance and diversity of species. |
| ALWW2 | Aquatic Life Warm Water-Class 2 | These are waters that are not capable of sustaining a wide variety of warm water biota, including sensitive species, due to physical habitat, water flows or levels, or uncorrectable water quality conditions that result in substantial impairment of the abundance and diversity of species. |
| DWS | Domestic Water Source | These surface waters are suitable or intended to become suitable for potable water supplies. After receiving standard treatment (defined as coagulation, flocculation, sedimentation, filtration, and disinfection with chlorine or its equivalent) these waters will meet Colorado drinking water regulations and any revisions, amendments, or supplements thereto. |
| RPC | Recreation Primary Contact | These surface waters are suitable or intended to become suitable for recreational activities in or on the water when the ingestion of small quantities of water is likely to occur. Such waters include but are not limited to those used for swimming, rafting, kayaking and water-skiing. |
| RSC | Recreation Secondary Contact | These surface waters are suitable or intended to become suitable for recreational uses on or about the water which are not included in the primary contact subcategory, including but not limited to fishing and other streamside or lakeside recreation. |

*Source*: EPA WQSDB (Version 3).

---

[3] Park hydrographic statistics in Table IV account only for those NHD hydrographic features with an assigned WBID. Not all NHD features (*e.g.*, canal/ditch) are waterbodies as defined above in the background section. Therefore, Table I hydrographic statistics may differ from Table IV.

## Table III. Utah-Designated Beneficial Use Definitions

| State - Designated Use Code | State-Designated Use | State-Designated Use Definition |
|---|---|---|
| 1C | Drinking Water Supply | Protected for domestic purposes with prior treatment by processes as required by the Utah Department of Health. |
| 2B | Secondary Contact (Recreation) | Protected for secondary contact recreation such as boating, wading, or similar uses. |
| 3A | Cold Water Game Fish | Protected for cold water species of game fish and other cold water aquatic life, including the necessary aquatic organisms in their food chain. |
| 3B | Warm Water Game Fish | Protected for warm water species of fish and other warm water aquatic life, including the necessary aquatic organisms in their food chain. |
| 4 | Agriculture | Protected for agricultural uses including crop irrigation and stock watering. |

*Source*: EPA WQSDB (Version 3).

**Table IV. State-Designated Beneficial Uses and Use Support Information**

| Segment Name/Description[2] | WBID (305b WBID)[3] | Miles (In Park) | Miles (Adjacent) | Shoreline Miles[4] | Acres (In Park) | Acres (Adjacent)[5] | AG | ALCW1 | ALWW2 | DWS | RPC | RSC | 1C | 2B | 3A | 3B | 4 |
|---|---|---|---|---|---|---|---|---|---|---|---|---|---|---|---|---|---|
| Mainstem of the Yampa River from a point immediately above the confluence with Lay Creek to the confluence with the Green River. | COLCLY02 (COLCLY02_8100) | 48.23 | | | 2.92 | | F | | F | F | F | | | | | | |
| All tributaries to the Yampa River including all wetlands, lakes, and reservoirs from a point immediately below the confluence with Lay Creek to a point immediately below the confluence with the Little Snake River. | COLCLY14 (COLCLY14_8100) | 230.98 | | | | | F | | F | | | F | | | | | |
| Mainstem of the Green River within Colorado (Moffatt County). | COLCLY19 (COLCLY19_7800) | 25.32 | | | 48.65 | | F | F | | F | F | | | | | | |
| All tributaries to the Green Rive in Colorado, including all wetlands, lakes and reservoirs, except for the specific listings in Segments 21 and 22; all tributaries to the Yampa River from a point immediately below the confluence with the Green River, except for the specific listings in segments 15 through 18. | COLCLY20 (COLCLY20_7800) | 74.28 | | | | | F | | F | | F | | | | | | |

13

Table IV cont.

| Segment Name/Description[2] | WBID (305b WBID)[3] | Miles (In Park) | Miles (Adjacent) | Shoreline Miles[4] | Acres (In Park) | Acres (Adjacent)[5] | State-Designated Uses and Use Support[1] | | | | | | | | | | |
|---|---|---|---|---|---|---|---|---|---|---|---|---|---|---|---|---|---|
| | | | | | | | AG | ALCW1 | ALWW2 | DWS | RPC | RSC | 1C | 2B | 3A | 3B | 4 |
| All tributaries to the White River, including all wetlands, lakes and reservoirs, from a point immediately above the confluence with Douglas Creek to the Colorado/Utah border, except for specific listing in Segment 23. | COLCWH22 (COLCWH22_8500) | 0.99 | | | | | NA | | NA | | NA | | | | | | |
| Green River and tributaries from confluence with Colorado River to State line, except. | UT-R-GREEN-0001 (UT14060001-001_00) | 140.18 | 13.95 | 0.5 | 4.68 | 535.61 | | | | | | | F | F | | | F |
| | | | | | | | | | | | | | | NA | | | F |
| Big Brush Creek and tributaries from confluence with Green River to Tyzack (Red Fleet) Dam. | UT-R-GREEN-0034 (UT14060002-003_00) | 0.95 | | | | | | | | | | | | NA | | F | F |
| Jones Hole Creek and tributaries from confluence with Green River to Headwaters. | UT-R-GREEN-0036 (UT14060001-002_00) | 6.33 | | | | | | | | | | | | NA | NA | F | NA |

*Sources*   *Regulation No. 37 – Classifications and Numeric Standards for Lower Colorado River Basin* (5 C.C.R. 1002-37); State of Colorado.  Colorado Department of Public Health and Environment – Water Quality Control Division. 2002a. *Status of Water Quality in Colorado*; and an extraction from Utah DEQ-DWQ's water quality standards database provided to the National Park Service in December 2002.

*Notes*
[1] Use Support Codes: F = Full support, T = Threatened, P = Partial support, N = Not supported, NA = Not assessed for use support.  Shaded rows have a use support designation of P or N.
[2] Segment Description was taken from Colorado water quality regulations.
[3] Some States use a different WBID for waters defined in their 305b reports than for waters defined in their water quality standards.  Depending on the State, the geographic extent of the 305b WBID (as compared to the water quality standard WBID) can be the same, can be a subset of, or can cover multiple WBIDs.
[4] Shoreline Miles applies to adjacent lakes/ponds, seas/oceans, swamps/marshes, reservoirs, or estuaries.
[5] Acres (Adjacent) applies only to the NHD 2-dimensional streams/rivers, which are represented in the NHD waterbody theme with polygons.

14

# WATER QUALITY CRITERIA

Water quality criteria for waterbodies within Colorado can be found in the Colorado Department of Public Health and Environment – Water Quality Control Division – Regulation No. 31 – *The Standards and Methodologies for Surface Water* located on the Internet at http://www.cdphe.state.co.us/op/regs/waterregs/100231.pdf. Criteria specific to those WBIDs within or adjacent to DINO can be found in the Colorado Department of Public Health and Environment – Water Quality Control Division – Regulation No. 37 – *Classification and Numeric Standards for Lower Colorado River Basin* located on the Internet at http://www.cdphe.state.co.us/op/regs/waterregs/100237wqcclowercoloradotables.pdf. Water quality criteria for waterbodies within Utah can be found in Utah's *Standards of Quality for Waters of the State* at R317-2-12 of the U.A.C. located on the Internet at http://www.rules.state.ut.us/publicat/code/r317/r317-002 htm.

# IMPAIRED WATERBODIES

Waterbodies with a use support designation of partial support or not supported are considered impaired for the purposes of 303(d) listing. No waterbodies within or adjacent to the DINO park boundary are impaired based on Colorado's 2002 (State of Colorado 2002b) or Utah's 2002 303(d) list (State of Utah 2002). WBIDs COLCLY02, COLCLY19, and COLCWH22 were, however, placed on Colorado's 2002 Monitoring and Evaluation (M&E) list for sediment, lead, and sediment, respectively (State of Colorado 2002b). Colorado's M&E list is used for those waterbodies where there is reason to suspect water quality problems, but there is uncertainty about their degree of use support (State of Colorado 2002a).

# TOTAL MAXIMUM DAILY LOAD

The TMDL program of the Clean Water Act provides the framework for identifying and restoring impaired waterbodies. This program requires TMDLs for all 303(d) listed waterbodies. A TMDL is a calculation of the maximum amount of a pollutant that a waterbody can receive and still meet water quality standards, and an allocation of that amount to the pollutant's sources (Environmental Protection Agency 2002a). No TMDL has been completed for a DINO waterbody.

# OUTSTANDING NATIONAL AND STATE RESOURCE WATERS

No ONRW (Tier 3) or Outstanding State Resource Waters (Tier 2 ½) have been applied to waters within or adjacent to the DINO park boundary in Colorado (5 C.C.R. 1002-37).

The following segments of the Green River Drainage within or adjacent to DINO have been designated as Category 1 (Tier 3) waters by the State of Utah (R317-2-12, U.A.C.):

> Jones Hole Creek and tributaries, from confluence with Green River to headwaters; and
> Green River, from state line to Flaming Gorge Dam.

**Figure 2. Waterbody Designated Uses and Impairment Status – Panel A**

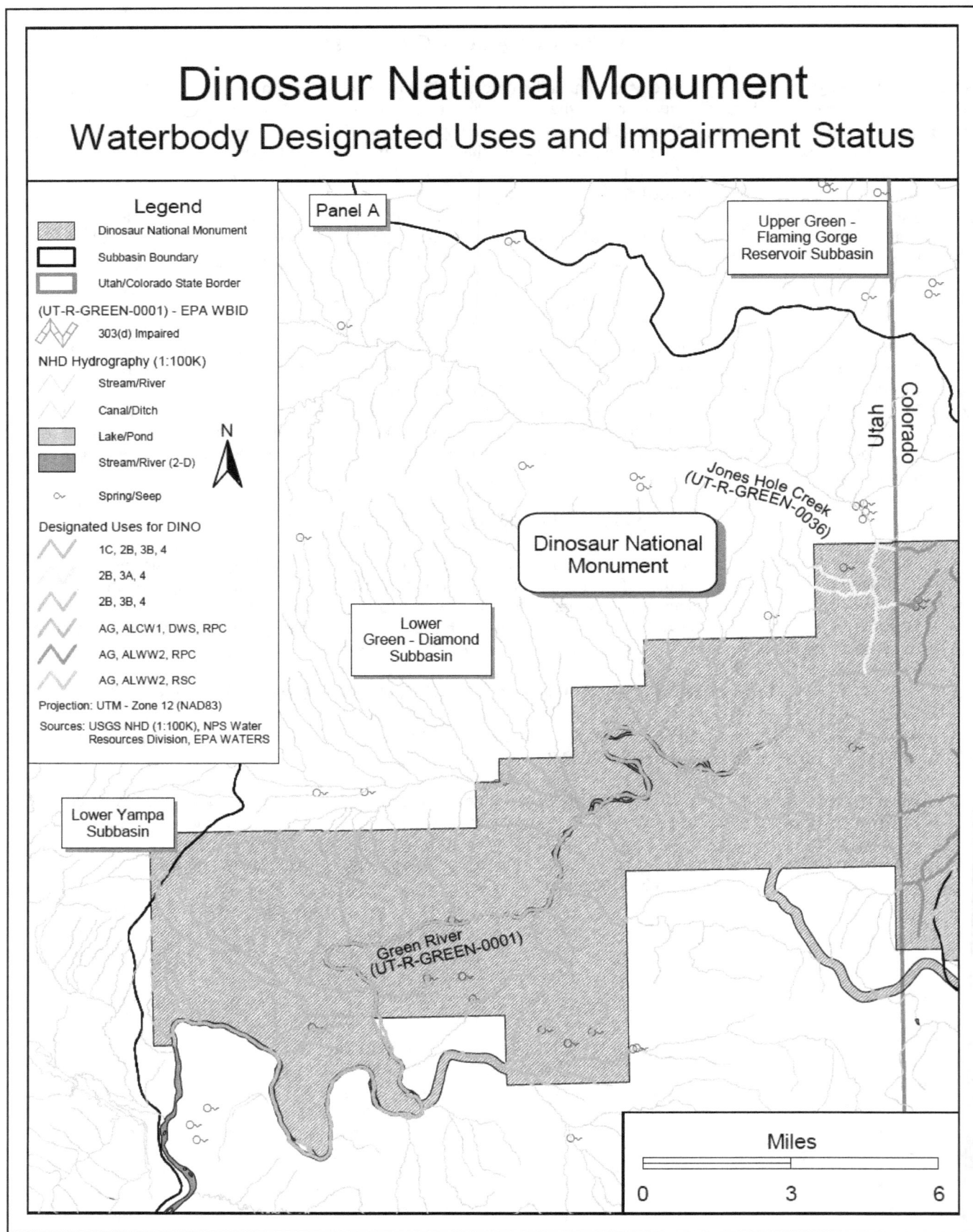

# Dinosaur National Monument
## Waterbody Designated Uses and Impairment Status

Legend

- Dinosaur National Monument
- Subbasin Boundary
- Utah/Colorado State Border

(UT-R-GREEN-0001) - EPA WBID
- 303(d) Impaired

NHD Hydrography (1:100K)
- Stream/River
- Canal/Ditch
- Lake/Pond
- Stream/River (2-D)
- Spring/Seep

N

Designated Uses for DINO
- 1C, 2B, 3B, 4
- 2B, 3A, 4
- 2B, 3B, 4
- AG, ALCW1, DWS, RPC
- AG, ALWW2, RPC
- AG, ALWW2, RSC

Projection: UTM - Zone 12 (NAD83)

Sources: USGS NHD (1:100K), NPS Water Resources Division, EPA WATERS

Panel A

Upper Green - Flaming Gorge Reservoir Subbasin

Utah | Colorado

Jones Hole Creek (UT-R-GREEN-0036)

Dinosaur National Monument

Lower Green - Diamond Subbasin

Lower Yampa Subbasin

Green River (UT-R-GREEN-0001)

Miles

0       3       6

Figure 3. Waterbody Designated Uses and Impairment Status – Panel B

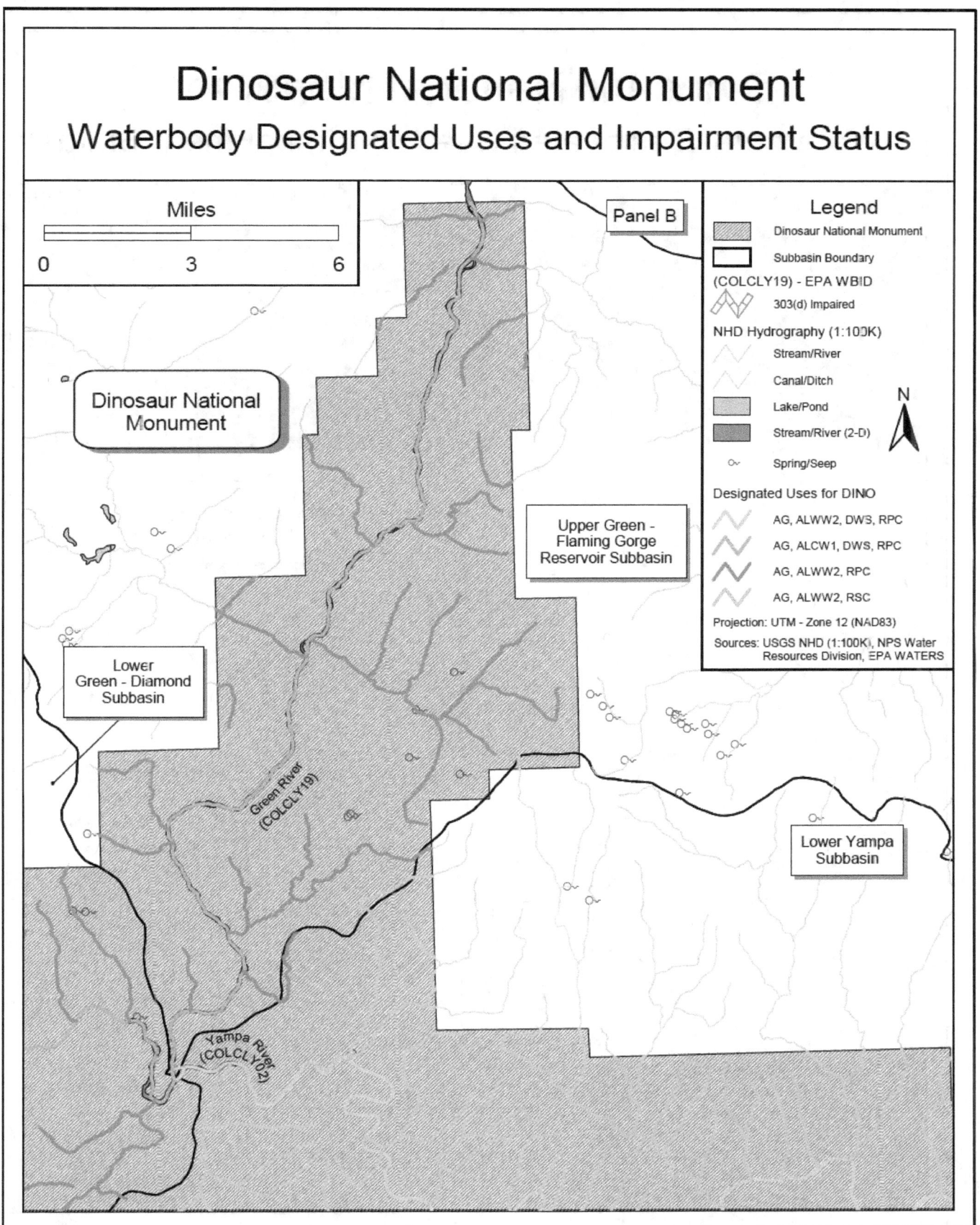

**Figure 4. Waterbody Designated Uses and Impairment Status – Panel C**

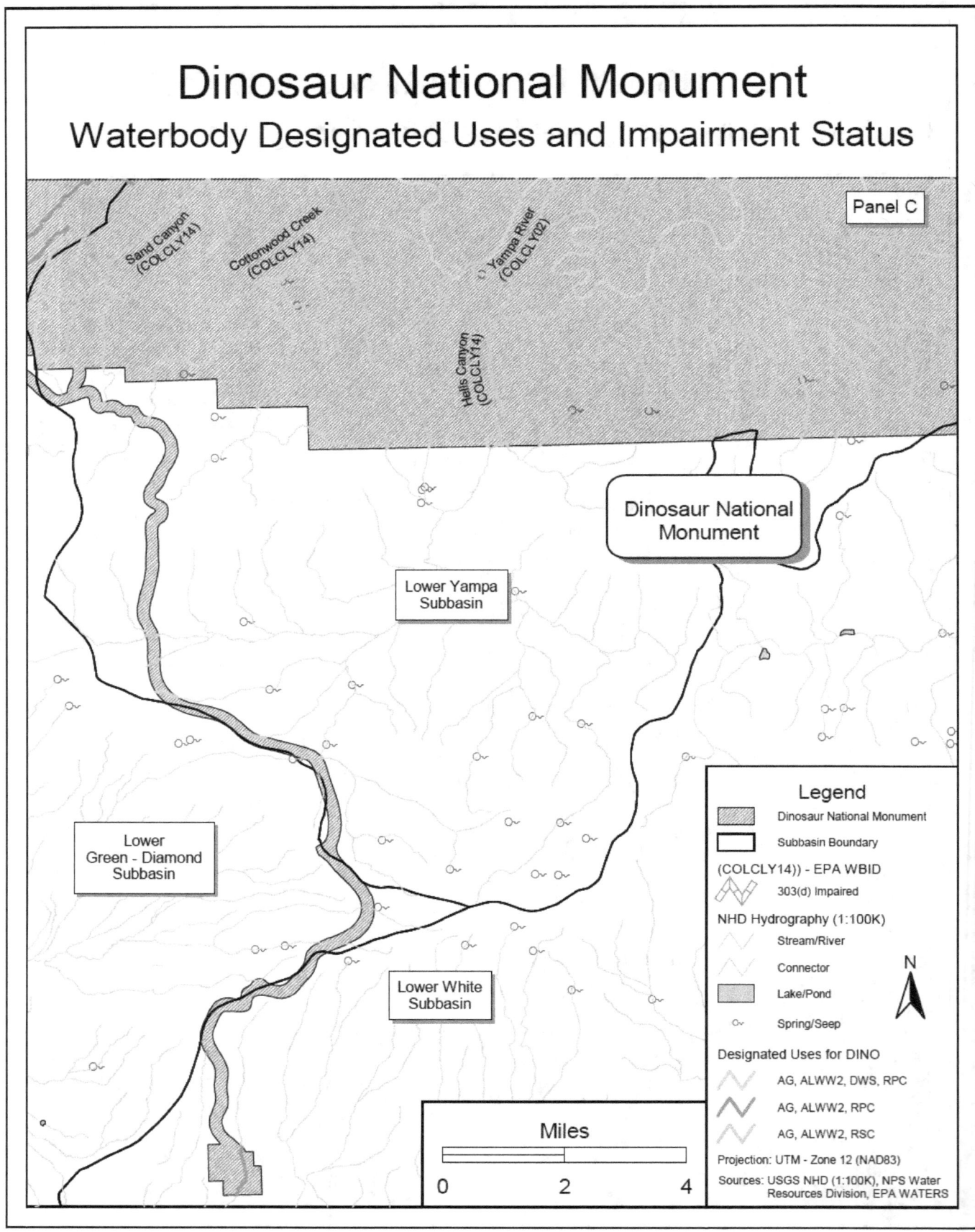

**Figure 5. Waterbody Designated Uses and Impairment Status – Panel D**

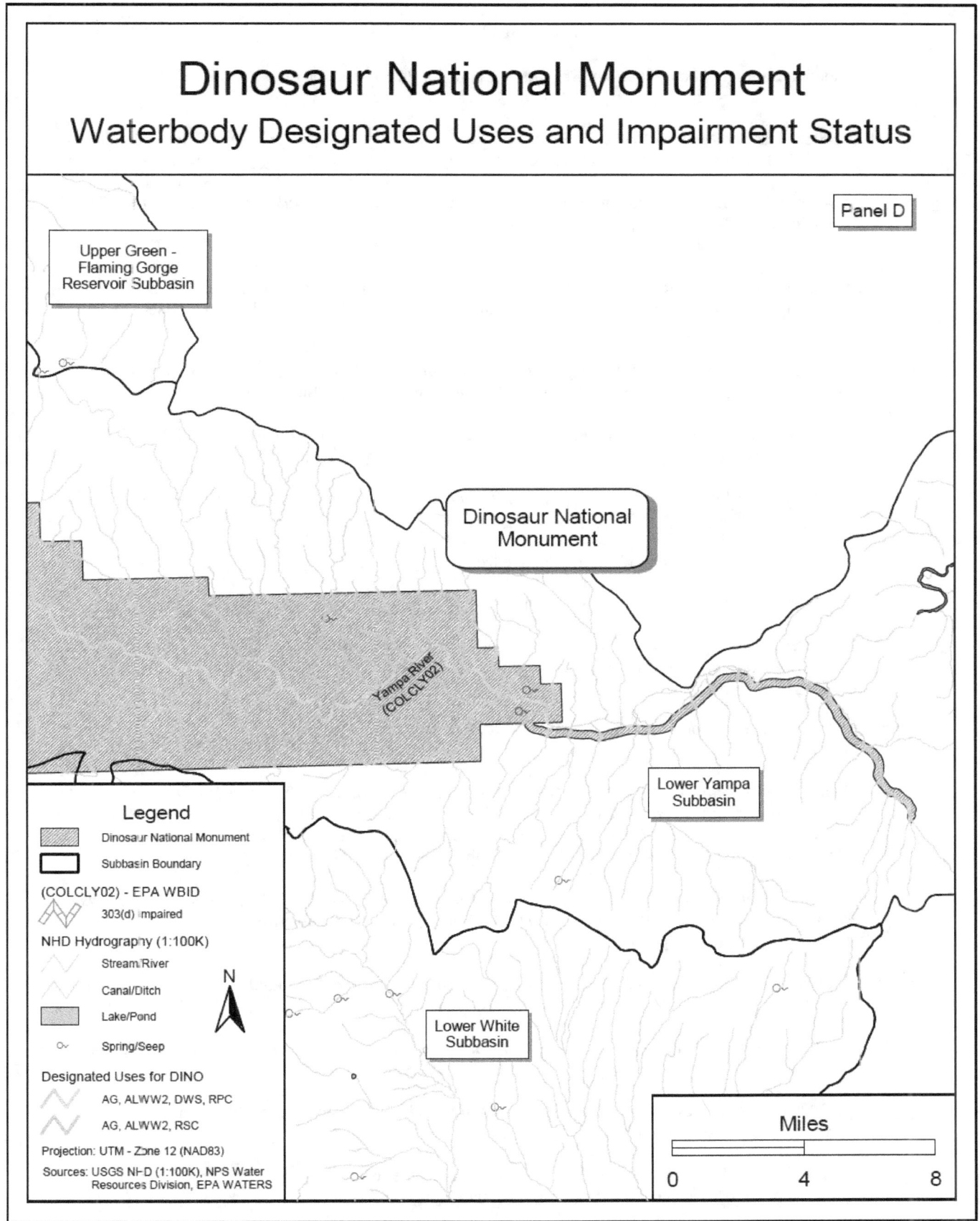

# LITERATURE CITED

"Antidegradation Policy." *Code of Federal Regulations* Title 40, Pt. 131.12, 2001 ed. Available from http://www.access.gpo.gov/nara/cfr/cfr-table-search html#page1.

"The Basic Standards and Methodologies for Surface Water." *Colorado Code of Regulations* Title 5, Regulation 1002-31 (30 October 2001). Available from http://www.cdphe.state.co.us/op/regs/waterregs/100231.pdf.

"Classifications and Numeric Standards for Lower Colorado River Basin." *Colorado Code of Regulations* Title 5, Regulation 1002-37 (30 August 2002). Available from http://www.cdphe.state.co.us/op/regs/waterregs/100237wqcclowercoloradotables.pdf.

"Congressional Declaration of Goals and Policy." *U.S.Code* Title 33, Section 1251(a). Quoted in Thomas F.P. Sullivan (ed.). 1995. *Environmental Law Handbook (13th ed.)*. 136. Rockville: Government Institutes, Inc.

Environmental Protection Agency. 1993. *Water Quality Standards Handbook – Second Edition* (Ch. 4 – Antidegradation). Washington, DC: Office of Water Regulations and Standards.

_____. 1998. *Water Quality Criteria and Standards Plan – Priorities for the Future*. EPA 822-R-98-003. Available from http://www.epa.gov/waterscience/standards/criplan615.pdf.

_____. 2001. *2002 Integrated Water Quality Monitoring and Assessment Report Guidance*. Available from http://www.epa.gov/owow/tmdl/2002wqma.pdf.

_____. 2002a. *Introduction to TMDLs*. Available from http://www.epa.gov/owow/tmdl/intro.html.

_____. 2002b. *Geography of* Waters. Available from http://www.epa.gov/waters/about/geography.html.

"EPA Administered permit programs: The national pollutant discharge elimination system – Definitions." *Code of Federal Regulations* Title 40, Pt. 122.2, 2001 ed. Available from http://www.access.gpo.gov/nara/cfr/cfr-table-search html#page1.

Gallagher, Lynn. M., and Leonard. A. Miller. 1996. *Clean Water Handbook (2nd ed.)*. Rockville: Government Institutes, Inc.

Galvin, Denis P. 1999. *Statement of Denis P. Galvin, Deputy Director, National Park Service, Department of the Interior, Before the Subcommittee on National Parks, Historic Preservation, and Recreation of the Senate Committee on Energy and Natural Resources, concerning the implementation of the Government Performance and Results Act*. Available from http://www nps.gov/legal/testimony/106th/gpra8499 htm.

General Accounting Office. 2002. *Water Quality: Inconsistent State Approaches Complicate Nation's Efforts to Identify Its Most Polluted Waters*. GAO-02-186 Water Quality. Available from http://www.epa.gov/waters/doc/gaofeb02.pdf.

National Park Service. 1992. *Natural Resources Inventory Monitoring Guideline*. Publication NPS-75. Available from http://www nature.nps.gov/nps75/nps75.pdf.

_____. 1993. *Strategic Plan for Conducting Level I Baseline Natural Resource Inventories in the National Park Service*.

_____. 2000a. *Natural Resource Inventory & Monitoring in National Parks*. Available from http://www.nature.nps.gov/im/brochure/imbroch htm.

_____. 2000b. *NPS Strategic Plan for FY 2001-2005*. Available from http://planning.den.nps.gov/document/NPS strategic plan.pdf.

"The National Park Service Organic Act."\* *U.S.Code* Title 16, Section 1, 2000 ed. Available from http://www.access.gpo.gov/uscode/uscmain.html. \* This title is not an official short title but merely a popular name used for the convenience of the reader.

"Revisions to the Water Quality Planning and Management Regulation and Revisions to the National Pollutant Discharge Elimination System Program in Support of Revisions to the Water Quality Planning and Management Regulation; Final Rule." *Federal Register* 65:135 (13 July 2000) p. 43588. Available from http://www.epa.gov/owow/tmdl/finalrule/finalrule.pdf.

River Network. State-by-State Antidegradation Information. Available from http://www.rivernetwork.org/library/librivcwa_antideg.htm#utah; accessed 24 September 2002.

State of Colorado. Colorado Department of Public Health and Environment – Water Quality Control Division. 1998. *Colorado Water Quality Management and Drinking Water Protection Handbook – A Continuing Planning Process*. Commission Policy #98-2. Expiration Date: December 31, 2002. Available from http://www.cdphe.state.co.us/op/wqcc/98-2.pdf.

_____. 2002a. *Status of Water Quality in Colorado*.

_____. 2002b. *Water Quality Limited Segments Still Requiring TMDLs – Colorado's 2002 303(d) List and Monitoring and Evaluation List*. Available from http://www.cdphe.state.co.us/op/wqcc/combo303dfinal.pdf.

"Standards of Quality for Waters of the State." *Utah Administrative Code* Rule R317-2 (1 July 2002). Available from http://www.rules.state.ut.us/publicat/code/r317/r317-002.htm.

Sullivan, Thomas F. P., ed. 1995. *Environmental Law Handbook (13th ed.)*, 139. Rockville: Government Institutes, Inc.

U.S. Geological Survey. 2000a. *Concepts and Contents: NHD Technical Reference*. Available from http://nhd.usgs.gov/chapter1/chp1_data_users_guide.pdf.

_____. 2000b. *Introducing the NHDinARC*. Available from http://nhd.usgs.gov/chapter2/IntroNHDinARC02_07.pdf.

As the nation's principal conservation agency, the Department of the Interior has the responsibility for most of our nationally owned public lands and natural and cultural resources. This includes fostering wise use of our land and water resources, protecting our fish and wildlife, preserving the environmental and cultural values of our national parks and historical places, and providing for enjoyment of life through outdoor recreation. The Department assesses our energy and mineral resources and works to ensure that their development is in the best interests of all our people. The Department also promotes the goals of the Take Pride in America campaign by encouraging stewardship and citizen responsibility for American Indian reservation communities and for people who live in island territories under U.S. administration.

NPS D-128                    March 2003